(2/6

ORDERS IN ORBIT

ORDERS IN ORBIT

S. J. FORREST

ILLUSTRATED BY

E. W. FORREST

LONDON

A. R. MOWBRAY & Co. LIMITED

First published in 1962

PRINTED IN GREAT BRITAIN BY
A. R. MOWBRAY & CO. LIMITED IN THE CITY OF OXFORD
2295

PREFACE

DOUBTLESS a poet might do worse
Than write his preface all in verse;
This, if the reader will allow,
Is simply what I'm doing now,
To greet my loyal friends, and true,
With just a gentle word or two.
If only I could answer some
Who question how the verses come;
But whence the unrelenting flow
I doubt if I shall ever know.
An urgent spate of flowing rhymes
Comes surging at the queerest times,
And none is more surprised than I
When driven on to versify.

At first they sold my verbal tricks
In pamphlets thin, at one-and-six,
(With paper backs of azure tint),
But these are wholly out of print.
Sir Mowbray, to revive their fame,
Undaunted to the rescue came,
And keenly laboured to produce
The rosy-coloured *What's the Use*,
Which Betjeman, a kindly friend,
Was sympathetic to commend.
There followed on, in season due,
Time for a Rhyme in coat of blue:
Chapter and Verse was number three,
In red and black all plain to see;
At last appeared, in lightish brown,
Town Parson's Day at half-a-crown.

Despite the sinister array,
The author's still at large to-day;
And, year by year, for good or ill,
Is perpetrating verses still.
There's always reason for a rhyme,
And scope for laughter all the time,
So this is why, you understand,
You hold his poems in your hand.
Thus may we hope this friendly chaff
Provokes a salutary laugh:
Down in the Forrest something stirred,
We trust it may not get the bird.

1962   S. J. F.

...A STRANGE PHENOMENON

ORDERS IN ORBIT

I KNOW a merry clergyman
　　Who's very very high,
It's hard to tell if he's on earth
　　Or orbiting the sky.

I know a gentle clergyman
　　Who's very very low,
But if he's here or underneath
　　It's difficult to know.

I know a kindly clergyman
　　Who's very very wide,
We cannot judge if he's within
　　Or somewhere far outside.

Yet all the three, with one accord,
  Infallibly agree,
To serve in simple loyalty
  Within the C. of E.

Some say the age of miracles
  Will never come again,
Yet here's a strange phenomenon
  That no one can explain.

ECCLESIA HYPODERMICA

'The child has not been baptized, but has received the triple protective inoculation.'
Extract from Official Report.

THOUGH world and flesh and Satan still
  Menace the path we tread,
The trine affusion we discard
  For threefold jab instead.

If triple prick admits the soul
  Into the realm of Heaven;
Would Confirmation thus require
  Inoculations seven?

With old scholastic pedantry
  Our problem lies conjoint—
How many Christians can alight
  Upon a needle's point?

And might we find an up-to-date
  System of Ordination,
By hypodermic syringe
  After careful calculation?

How speedy the reunion
  Ecumenists will wish up
When they can say how many jabs
  Suffice to make a Bishop!

...TO MAKE A BISHOP

... CALL ME HANK

ABBREVIATED ABBESS

'Wearing a workman's cap inscribed "Hank," Mother Henry of the Sisters of . . .
U.S.A., is acting as foreman on building works at the Convent. . . .'—*News item*.

SAID Mother Henry to her nuns,
'This precedence, or rank,
Is contrary to sisterhood,
In future call me Hank.
I mean to wear a workman's cap
To publicize my name,
And every sister in the house
Shall likewise do the same.

'Let Sister Florence now be Floss,
And Sister Bertha, Bert,
Hippolyta reduce to Hip,
And Gertrude down to Gert.
Call Sister Ethelburga Eth,
Let Dorothy be Dot,
While dear old dim Clothild becomes,
Appropriately, Clot.
Loquacious Gabrielle is Gab,
Lettice appears as Let,
And, as for sweet Perpetua,
She's always been our Pet.
Let Sister Catherine arise
As queen of all the Cats,
Though Sister Bathild must remain
Inevitably Bats.

'So every Sister shall display
Her name upon her cap,
And will, in future, designate
The Chapel as her Chap.
As we upon our scaffolding
Gymnastically romp,
Building our ultra-modern Conv.,
All day from Matt., till Comp.,
A shortie habit I'll design
Appropriate to this,
And every one shall call me Mum,
And I shall call you Sis.'

SACRED COW

'Wanted: Man and woman to look after two cows, both Protestant.'

Advert in Ulster paper

PROTESTANT cows,
  Won't milk on Sundays,
Puritan cows,
  Are dubious of mud;
Baptist cows,
  Get immersed in the waterways,
Anglican cows,
  Chew overmuch cud.
Romanist cows,
  Need plenary indulgence,
Methodist cows,
  Refuse barley and hops;
Adventist cows,
  Take a rest on Saturdays,
Orthodox cows,
  Are omphalloscopes.

Cows Unitarian,
  Boggle at the clover,
Genevan Calvinists,
  Dislike lucerne;
Clairvoyant cows,
  Have a yield only medium,
Lutheran cows,
  Are faithful, but stern.
Salvation cows,
  Always trumpet like an elephant,
Brawly the cow Presbyterian,
  Hoots!
Strict and Particular,
  Low as they make 'em,
Quakers are silent,
  But friendly old brutes.

Thus, as the middlemen
    Come for the marketing,
Readily prepared
    With a number of churns,
Keeping the Catholic milk
    From the Protestant,
Lest in a quantity
    The aggregate turns.
All this variety
    Of vaccine devotion,
Poses a problem
    Experiment must solve:
Breeding the beast
    For the triumph of reunion,
How may the paragon
    Lactiferous evolve?

How can we fashion
    The cow Ecumenical,
Worthy of leaping
    The moon at the full?
Surely by crossing
    The Protestant varieties
With an acceptable and strong
    Papal Bull.

... PAPAL BULL

GOOD EGG

It has been suggested that the Easter Egg might have proved a more suitable emblem of Christianity than the Cross.

HE asked me to visit his modernized church,
  With an ovoid surmounting the spire;
So I followed behind the processional egg,
  And a totally bald-headed choir.

The church in itself has an oviform plan,
  With everything set in the round;
And symbolic eggs in impressive array,
  Where a cross would be normally found.

Though incense is sternly prohibited here,
  Or fragrance of foliage gay,
The boiler diffuses a sulphurous fume,
  Like an egg that has finished its day.

A hard-boiled and stubborn minority group
  Who sit in the gallery pews,
Are finding the egg a convenient way
  Of stressing dissentient views.

He showed me the font in the form of a nest,
  I thought he was pulling my leg,
When he told me that every child he baptized,
  Was signed with the Sign of the Egg.

. . . MODERNIZED CHURCH

The egg, he considered an emblem supreme,
   For modern and sceptical thought;
Requiring no more than the slightest of change,
   To make it the Sign of the Nought.

Quite soon, we imagine, he'll answer the call,
   As bishop of some neo-Zion,
Displaying a glorious pectoral Egg,
   With the stamp of the Anglican Lion.

SEMI-REV.

'Half priests, half laymen.'—Headline in Church newspaper.

I MET a schizoid fantasy,
    Upon a winter's day,
One half of him was clerical,
    The other half was lay.

'It's something of a tragedy,'
    He said, in accents pained,
'When I was made a deacon,
    I was only half-ordained.

'The Bishop had an accident,
    Or so I understand,
And, since his arm was in a sling,
    Could only use one hand.

'Which left me with a horrid fear
    Persisting night and day
That half of me was clerical,
    The other being lay.

'I know I look a funny sight
    To anybody's eye,
With half a collar in reverse,
    And half a college tie.

'Yet clergymen and laity
    Unite in me,' he smiled,
'Traditional antagonists
    Completely reconciled!

... COMPLETELY RECONCILED

'In future schemes for Unity,
I shouldn't be surprised,
Some place for semi-presbyters
Will doubtless be devised.'

FEET OF CLAY

' 'Tıs very nearly Christmastide,'
  Said Mum, in mid-November,
'This time last year, old Santa Claus
  Paraded, I remember.
We'll take young Joey to the shops
  To see the decorations.
We're sure to have a deal of fun
  Hearing his exclamations.'

Within the City's finest store,
  They saw a mighty wonder:
Great Father Christmas on his throne,
  Like Jove without his thunder.
A form of monumental size,
  Though not the least alarming,
Surmounted by a silken wig,
  All glamorous and charming.

'It's Santa Claus, come down to earth,'
  Said Mum to little Joey,
'See all the reindeer by his sledge,
  This scenery all snowy.'
So, as she watched his childish glee
  And gestures animated,
While Father Christmas he surveyed,
  His verdict she awaited.

A hush fell on the crowded store,
     All noisy talk abating,
As Joey made, in accents shrill,
     His comment devastating;
And every ear was turned to hear
     The words of this little laddie:
'He's wearing dirty old flannel bags,
     Exactly like my Daddy.'

... EXACTLY LIKE MY DADDY

USES OF DIVERSITY (A.D. 2000)

'Morning Service according to the Methodist Use; Evensong from the *Book of Common Prayer.*'—*Press report on a new district church.*

REFORMING zeal decreed of old,
  Mid warring rites, a truce,
Ordaining (with a childlike hope),
  'This Realm shall have one Use.'

Yet now the modern church recalls
  The Woman in her Shoe,
We have so many usages
  We don't know what to do.

Our active Rector strives to find,
  By comprehensive search,
How many uses he may cram
  Into a single church.

Since every sect in Whittaker
  Is safely gathered in,
Each Sunday we must now select
  Our usage with a pin.

Repulsing drab monotony,
  We find a goal unique:
Kaleidoscopic services,
  Entirely new each week.

... KALEIDOSCOPIC SERVICES

And spiky servers who discussed
   How Rome with Sarum vies,
Have uses multitudinous
   On which to exercise.

Thus, antiquated ritualists
   Will reap untold abuse,
For clinging to the outworn tag:
   'This Realm shall have one Use.'

LEG PULL

In a TV interview it was revealed that the Dean of Canterbury had devised a form of zip-fastener for dignitaries' gaiters.

THE Church, accused of many crimes,
And notably 'behind the times,'
May well acclaim her parent See
The hive of true modernity.

For here decanal notions bring
Relief to human suffering,
And none can say the Church's grip
Is lacking either zest or zip.

This blushing Dean in worthy pride,
Who fixed the zippers down the side,
Delights that gaiter'd souls arise
Free from the button's tyrannies.

Full many a bishop's heart has sunk
As from the grim ordeal he shrunk,
As bitter as a poison'd cup,
The task of doing gaiters up.

Archdeacons, too, were prone to quail,
On hearing the recurrent tale,
That once the wearer was inside,
He wore his gaiters till he died.

While many a giant turns to flee
The offer of a famous See,
And *nol' episcopari* begs
In mortal fear of gaiter'd legs.

But now the gaiter's lost its sting,
A harmless inoffensive thing.
With many a joke and lightsome quip,
Each dignitary jerks his zip.

Archdeacons, in the morning bright,
Zip up the left, zip up the right,
As each with facile motion grabs
His Canterbury zipper-tabs.

'Pull up your socks,' the people say,
(The *Sursum Corda* of to-day),
But now the phrase must supervene
'Zip up your gaiters, Mr. Dean.'

... JERKS HIS ZIP

AS PANTS

A BOOK on ceremonial
   Provokes a noted jest,
By ordering the celebrant
   To 'wash his hands and vest.'

At our young curate's idle ways
   The Vicar storms and rants,
Who, coming to the vestry late,
   Washes his hands and pants.

DISTANT BRAY

In Bishop Barnes's spacious days,
    When Modernists campaign'd, Sir,
I followed in the current craze,
    In Birmingham ordain'd, Sir.
        We strove to storm
        The ancient form
    With conscience all elastic,
        And jettison'd
        All dogma fond,
    In zeal iconoclastic.

Chorus: Th' Establishment,
            I can't resent,
        While this shall be my joy, Sir,
            That, come what may,
            I mean to stay,
        The Bishop's blue-eyed boy, Sir.

But times must move, and bishops too,
    As fashions grew liturgic,
        To endless range
        Of ritual change
    I never prov'd allergic.
        By facing West,
        With all the rest
    I found it so much better;
        My sterile rite
        Suggesting quite
    An operating theatre.

Chorus: Th' Establishment
            Brings me content
        Which nothing can destroy, Sir,
            And, come what may,
            I mean to stay
        The Bishop's blue-eyed boy, Sir.

...EXOTIC PARISH DINNERS

When bishops ecumenical,
   Were zealous for reunion
And quite prepared to sacrifice
   The Anglican Communion,
     I ceas'd to praise
     The ancient ways
That in the C. of E. are,
     That every sect,
     Might recollect
They're just as good as we are.

Chorus: Th' Establishment,
                  Wins my assent,
              And brings me ceaseless joy, Sir,
                  For, come what may,
                  I mean to stay
              The Bishop's blue-eyed boy, Sir.

          But now financial consciousness
              Has dawn'd upon our masters,
          And stewardship campaigns involve
              Both laity and pastors:
                  I've bought a book,
                  And learnt to cook,
              Exotic parish dinners,
                  And therefrom trawl
                  A record haul
          From all my saints and sinners.

Chorus: Th' Establishment
                  I represent
              My talents shall employ, Sir,
                  So, come what may,
                  I mean to stay,
              The Bishop's blue-eyed boy, Sir!

... A QUASI-POPE

QUASIMODO

'We shall continue to keep the Sunday after Corpus Christi as of a quasi-octave.'
Announcement by a Parish Priest.

THE modern quasi-presbyter
 And every quasi-priest,
Must use a quasi-calendar
 Of quasi-fast and feast.

We keep, within our parish church,
 A wide variety
Of festivals, some quasi-Rome,
 Some quasi-B.C.P.

This quasi-Corpus Christi-tide,
  We now observe in church,
Has lost its quondam octave-day,
  And swept us from our perch.

How can we keep an almanack
  Within our sacred home,
One half by Cranmer bowdlerized,
  The other half by Rome?

Yet, since we're very often known
  As quasi-Catholics,
We unashamedly provide
  A super quasi-mix.

Experimental liturgy
  Shall never be absurd,
If *quasi* be allowed to stay
  The operative word.

And reconciling opposites
  Would be a slender hope,
Without the parish clergyman
  Who is a quasi-pope.

THE MARTYR

GOOD Father Q believed himself a martyr for the right
The bishops he'd resisted were too numerous to cite,
Full many persecutions he had suffered at their hand,
A record, quite undoubtedly the highest in the land.

Secure within the fortress of his freehold he would cry,
'All hideous erastians I finally defy;
My protestant diocesans may fulminate or ban,
The only Bishop I approve is in the Vatican.'

By adamant intransigeance, withstanding every blow,
As bishop after bishop did his best to bring him low,
He gained the reputation of a veritable rock,
With fortitude impregnable repelling every shock.

For years and years uncountable he'd confidently boast,
'I've fought a pretty battle with the Calvinistic host;
Resisting many bishops in a devastating war,
And even looking forward to defying many more.'

One day a new diocesan invited Father Q
To come and tell him candidly the things he wished to do.
So, with grimly set expression and a tightly clenching fist,
He cited in defiance every item on the list,
Depicting, like an artist in the gaudiest of paints,
The tabernacles, monstrances, and relics of the saints;
And arrogantly emphasized the things he valued most,
The Rosary, our Lady and processions of the Host.

The bishop listened carefully, and told him on the spot,
'If you believe all this is good, O.K., then, have the lot!
And now our happy conference must very quickly end,
For I have other clergymen to interview, my friend.'

'Good bye,' his Lordship added, 'and I hope we shortly meet.'
But Father Q sat motionless and rigid in his seat;
For, paralysed and overwrought by what had just been said,
The thought of approbation by a bishop struck him dead.

... RIGID IN HIS SEAT

... DUAL PERSONALITY

QUIT SPLIT

'In the interests of symmetry the choir will make their exit by both north and south doors of the church.'—*Parish magazine.*

THE animals came in two by two,
But they never went out the way we do.
Our choir now suddenly divides
And makes an exit through both sides.
A rending sight it is to see
This symbol of disunity;
Which damage we, of course, repair
By a stereophonic vestry prayer.

To mar the Rector's plan devout,
He finds himself the odd man out;
Somehow to split himself in two
He is beside himself to do.
For, future priests will need to be
Of dual personality,
And thus we'll see on either side,
The Reverend Jekyll and Father Hyde.

NUN UP

THE story is told at a convent in France
Concerning a sister, who oft, in a trance,
Would suddenly levitate high in the air,
Remaining aloft in an ecstasy there.
This manifestation that none could gainsay,
Embarrassed the sisters for many a day;
With frequent discussion and anxious debate,
They sought to explain her remarkable state.
The general trend of opinion was sure
The sister had come to a sanctity pure,
And freed from the gravity, burden, and taint
Of cumbering sin, she'd arisen a saint.
The Reverend Mother, the sisters all knew,
Was loath to agree to the general view,
A facile solution she couldn't embrace,
Till expert opinion should settle the case.

It happened one day, in the middle of None,
The sister in question emitted a groan,
(The sign which announced these phenomena strange),
Completed her count-down, and launched from the range;
And only the beautiful ceiling on high
Prevented her flight to the uttermost sky,
For, had not the celure retained her in place,
She might have arrived at an orbit in space.
That day, it transpired that a worthy old priest
Had come to the convent to help at the feast,
And entered the chapel precisely in time
To witness her non-gravitational climb.

C

The Mother appealed to this counsellor wise,
Inquired if he knew why the sister should rise;
Was such levitation a marvellous sign
Denoting a sanctity wholly divine?
How happy the sisters would certainly feel
Could this be confirmed by a heavenly seal.
The chaplain stood solemnly lost in his thought,
Revolving in mind what experience taught,
He offered no comment, revealed no surprise,
But turned to the nuns with a smile in his eyes,
And said, in a whimsical murmur, and sweet,
'The darling old sister has *very* big feet!'

The nun, who had heard this aside from the priest,
Came down with a bump, and exploded, 'You beast!'
No sputnik, or satellite, strange to relate,
Re-entered the air in so heated a state,
The strings of invective she fiercely unfurled,
Were something derived from a different world,
Reviving full many a picturesque phrase
That life in a convent had failed to erase,
A sad exhibition to shock and appal,
And each of the sisters bowed low in her stall.
So, none was amazed when the priest in a trice
Delivered his verdict succinct and precise:
'You asked me to judge if I thought her a saint,
Well, to put it quite simply, if crudely, SHE AIN'T.'

. . . VERY BIG FEET

. . . KIDNAPPING

THE SNATCH

'An undesirable practice of enticing away assistant priests from their parishes.'
Letter in Church Press.

RECURRENT weekly wages raids,
By dastard gangs in ambuscades,
Are nothing to the gory fights
Of curate snatchers, Sunday nights.

For curates now have come to be
The rarest *animalculae*,
And everywhere throughout the land,
Are in a desperate demand.

Curate-starvation thus transmutes
Pathetic vicars into brutes,
Who plot and artfully conspire
To trap the colleagues they require.

With clandestine, nocturnal stealth,
They stalk the parishes of wealth,
That can a curate's stipend pay,
And whisk the clergymen away.

Their nylon-stocking masks they don,
And, in a vast pantechnicon,
A grimly ruthless task perform
With coshes, ropes and chloroform.

The deaneries are now imbued
With something like a tribal feud,
And rural deans themselves are known
To go kidnapping on their own.

Vicars, beware the double speech
Of clergymen who come to preach;
Remember this important point,
They may be there to case the joint.

So, when you shut the house at night,
Put out the cat and dowse the light,
Make all secure with double locks,
And chain your curate in a box.

OLD VIC

IF people writing to my home,
    (Once commented the Vicar),
Paid more attention how they spell,
    I'd get their letters quicker.

The parsonage, or residence,
    At which you find me dwelling,
Is Vicar*age*, not Vicar-idge,
    By customary spelling.

. . . THE VIXENESS

With double Cs and double Ks,
   Or C plus K we're smitten,
And Viccar, Vikker, Vickerage,
   Are ignorantly written.

Yet there are times, I must admit,
   When, working like a nigger,
My vanity is gratified
   When designated Viggar.

But, though I'm fond of licorice,
   And not averse to liquor,
My wife is NOT the Vicorice,
   And I am not the Viquor.

For, both of us expect our friends
   To think of something nicer,
Than terming her the Vixeness
   Or calling me the Vicer.

SIM-NELL CAKE

SIMON and Nellie on Mothering Sunday,
  Hoping to give all the children a treat,
Rummage the larder, the previous Monday,
  Find it contains insufficient to eat.

Flour, their only available forage,
  Which into dough they are able to make;
With an admixture of stale currant porridge;
  How shall they cook this remarkable cake?

'Dough,' comments Nellie, 'is fit for the ovens,'
  'Porridge,' says Simon, 'is certainly not,
So by the law that our cookery governs,
  This composition should stew in the pot!'

Thus, in crescendo the argument crosses,
  Voices increase to the pitch of a scream,
Her wooden spoon on his tender proboscis,
  Alters his physiognomical scheme.

Compromise quickly inspires a decision
  Firstly to boil it, and finally bake;
So is begun an impressive tradition
  Mothering Sunday's delectable cake.

So were the parents and children contented
  Learning to boil it and bake it as well
Thus, in a cake, was a household cemented
  Joining the names of old Simon and Nell.

...AN IMPRESSIVE TRADITION

Marzipan now is the coating external
  Taking the place of original crust;
Sweetmeat adorable, nearly supernal,
  Still for the festal occasion a 'must'!

Still, on this day of exceptional bonhomie,
  Mothers are filled with legitimate pride;
Fathers rejoice in a pleasant gastronomy,
  Filled with the cake that tradition supplied.

... MAINTAINING EQUILIBRIUM

AVERSION TO CONVERSION

'The Church of England has always discouraged the making of converts.'
From an article in the Press.

'I SHAN'T convert you, for, you see,
I'm very strictly C. of E.
My doctrine cannot make you chafe,
For it is all entirely safe.
My sermons, too, will give you joy,
Containing nothing to annoy,
Contrived to be completely true
To each conflicting point of view,
With pros and cons in equal sum
Maintaining equilibrium;
With every statement qualified,
By quoting from the other side.'

'The pregnant phrase of good St. Paul
I make my own, "All things to all,"
And claim that white implies the black,
Each front a corresponding back,
That every colour that is true
Involves a complementary hue,
That truth may be combined with lies
By means of skilful compromise.
No discipline will I suggest
To cause discomfort or unrest,
No propagandist wares purvey,
No challenges to give dismay;
And no unsanctified delights
In hypnotizing proselytes.'

'So, if you start to go my way
It is in spite of what I say,
Not otherwise, for we must be
A *gentlemanly* C. of E.'

ARSON BY THE PARSON

Our Vicar's pyromania, extravagant and rash,
Has rendered a beloved Church to heaps of blackened ash.
Though adequate insurances will put us on our feet,
We shiver in the parish room, each Sunday, as we meet.

We never could appreciate his pyrotechnic games,
When lighting up the chancel, with innumerable flames
Of candles on the reredos, the altar, and the choir,
A veritable fantasy of incandescent fire.

We felt it was imperative a special fund to raise
To buy asbestos clothing to protect us from the blaze.
'It signifies the Light of Heaven,' the Vicar used to tell,
But we agreed it symbolized the other place as well.

One day (*he* called it Candlemas), the tragedy occurred:
He planned a festival of light or something quite absurd,
And, in the long procession, as it moved towards the door,
The choristers were spilling blobs of wax upon the floor;
So trying to correct them and to put their candles right,
The Vicar set his surplice accidentally alight.

This reverend incendiary, bursting into flame,
A strikingly illuminating spectacle became;
And, in our modest estimate, agreeing with the rest,
Was seen on this occasion at his brightest and his best.

But six intrepid gentlemen who followed with the choir
Abandoning their candlesticks, attempt to dowse the fire;
Apply their heavy music-books with resonating thwack,
And castigate the Vicar at the front and at the back.

To mar this most impressive of remarkable escapes,
Some ass had left his lighted torch recumbent on the drapes,
To start a conflagration and to burn the building down,
Thus making sure that Candlemas was kept throughout the town.

We grumbled to the Bishop, who replied, 'You must agree,
Your Vicar is precisely as you wanted him to be;
For when about the vacancy I ventured to inquire,
You wrote: "Please send a clergyman with lots and lots of fire." '

... A CLERGYMAN WITH LOTS AND LOTS OF FIRE

. . . A WAVE OF HIS HAND

PAX ROMANA

THROUGH forty years they waged the war
   Against the clerical foe,
And swore that the popish practices
   Would certainly have to go.

They vowed to expel the statuary,
   And the trumpery idols of Rome,
And banish elaborate candlesticks
   From their outraged spiritual home.

Till, at last with a faculty well in hand,
   They were able to overthrow
The final papistical ornaments,
   And restore the *status quo*.

And thus they did the self-same thing,
   In the forty years they planned,
That the Pope's own bishop in Aberdeen,
   Achieved with a wave of his hand.

...THE DAY WHEN I HEARD ABOUT HELL

EX ORE

A TEACHER was showing her children the Creed,
To clarify terms was her primary need;
The meaning of many she managed to tell,
But found herself stuck at the phrase about Hell,
(Which doesn't apply to the punishment dread,
But means, in this context, the Place of the Dead.)
So, tentatively, she inquired if the word
Was one that her children had formerly heard.

'Oh, yes!' said a bright little infant of six,
'When Mummy was making a fire with some sticks
She lighted her hand, and came out with a yell,
And that was the day when I heard about Hell.'

REVEALED TREWTH

At an agricultural conference in Russia it was suggested that those who picked less than their allotted amount of cotton should be made to wear shorter trousers, so that 'people will know that they obtained smaller harvests.'

OUR wideawake Diocesan
    Inviting repercussions,
Has graded parsons on a scale
    Invented by the Russians.

An indicator he's evolved
    Ingeniously clever,
To show each clergyman's success
    In 'Stewardship' endeavour.

For purpose of encouragement,
    Or salutary caution,
Each must display a trouser-leg
    In suitable proportion.

'The longer legs your trews display,'
    His Lordship has directed,
'Will manifest the quantity
    In offerings collected.'

Thus at the winter conference,
    By means unprecedented,
The pantaloons, or football shorts,
    Their balance sheet presented.

Those flowing concertina-pants
    That trailed across the flooring,
Were sported by the bishop's fans
    Most zealous and adoring.

In netherwear voluminous,
    The diocese's backers
Proclaimed, by means of ample slacks,
    That they were not the slackers.

And, as the most expansive bags
    Displayed successful winners,
So here and there the hairy legs
    Revealed the hardened sinners.

Thus, as he watched with mounting pride,
    His best financial slickers,
The Bishop noted with dismay
    Too many vicars' knickers.

I wasn't at the conference,
    Although I'm not a 'meanie,'
But I've evaded 'stewardship,'
    And haven't a bikini.

We trust that bishops won't attempt,
    (Inspired by student ragging),
To frame a future Canon Law
    For clerical de-bagging.

FUNNY GOINGS-ON

'We had such a funny minister at our Church on Sunday, he asked us to be silent and think about our sins; I mean you don't do that kind of thing in the Church of England.'—*Comment in the village street.*

A VERY funny minister has come to serve our Church,
And, though I wouldn't say a word his morals to besmirch,
He isn't very healthy in his attitude to sin,
A topic that oppresses him and poisons him within.
For, when he takes a service and refers to human taint,
He ought to treat the matter with discretion and restraint,
And, if he thinks us sinners he should handle us with tact,
We find it rather grim to be reminded of the fact;
    Not telling us to probe inside, our wickedness to see,
    I mean, you don't behave like that within the C. of E.

Our very funny minister has also found a way
Of questioning the people on the money that they pay,
He reckons we should follow the example of the Jews,
And give a tithe of income as our customary dues.
It's really most impertinent, we find it pretty tough,
The forms from Inland Revenue are surely quite enough.
So, when he brings his envelopes, we all propose to strike
In favour of the principle of paying what we like.
    Religion in this country should be given to us free;
    I mean, you don't behave like that within the C. of E.

This most amazing minister has also got a craze
That everyone's religion should apply to seven days;
Yet only an eccentric, a fanatic, or a freak,
Would try to be religious in the middle of the week.
He constantly exhorts us to assist in parish work,
And says that social witness is a duty none may shirk;
A plausible suggestion, but a fiddle, I'm afraid,
For, after all, the parish is the job for which *he's* paid.
   So why should we perform the task for which he gets the fee;
I mean, you don't behave like that within the C. of E.

. . . ATTITUDE TO SIN

... FROM BABYLON

FISHY

A protestant organization has circulated a pamphlet warning the clergy that the Bishop's mitre is the fish head-dress of a Babylonian sea-god.

It came upon me as a shock,
(Although my nerves are firm as rock),
To know my venerable bish,
Was masquerading as a fish.
Yet now I realize why I squirm
Before his presence as a worm.

I used to think that his attire
Betokened pentecostal fire,
The pointed head-dress of the same
Suggesting cloven tongues of flame,
But little thought that he would don
A fish's head from Babylon.

And even if he comes bedight
In motley robes of black and white
His garb will plainly symbolize
What Shakespeare knew as Maggot-Pies,
A fowl by ancients known to be
The sign of baleful augury.

When magpies pass, tradition states,
One may avert the evil fates
By swiftly turning from the sight,
And smartly spitting to the right:
A ritual for all who fear,
The sight of rochet and chimere.

Suspicion falls, we must admit,
On every item of his kit;
Inviting thus a jaundiced view
Of shovel hats and gaiters too,
Which riding-habit typifies
The demon Huntsman of the skies.

And though these studies may assist
And fascinate the folklorist,
No simple cleric should forget
To wear a potent amulet,
Who spies, below the gaitered knees,
The hooves of Mephistopheles.

... FRONT AND SIDES AND BACK

INQUISITION

They badgered me intensively
  About my way of life,
They probed into my income
  And the earnings of my wife.
They questioned me about the fate
  Of every penny spent,
Each membership subscription
  Or donation that I sent:
They grilled me unrelentingly
  Beneath a glaring light,
Bombarding me with queries
  Every morning moon and night;
They fitted me with thumbscrews
  And they stretched me on the rack,
And ripped up all my pockets
  At the front and sides and back ...

'Twas NOT the Inland Revenue,
  I really should explain;
But only what the Vicar called
  'A Stewardship Campaign.'

... FOOTGEAR RESIDENTIAL

NEO NURSERY RHYME

'A reader returned from overseas was asked by the Income Tax authorities whether he had in the last four years "maintained a residence as a place of abode." Being uncertain what this meant he sought guidance ... he has now been asked whether he had "retained accommodation for occupation." '—*Peterborough in the 'Daily Telegraph.'*

A VENERABLE matriarch
      in footgear residential,
Bewildered by a multitude
      of infants pestilential,
Supplied a tasty bouillon
      for diet efficacious,
Devoid of any aggregate
      of matter farinaceous.
Then, after castigation
      in appropriate position,
Despatched the total complement
      to premature dormition.

... DARK APOSTOLICAN CURSE

DIM DOOM

'In terms of *Apostolican Curse*.'—*From a letter in the Press on the papal bull* Apostolicae Curae.

I READ in a notable tome,
  (We study for better or worse),
Of a hideous threat to my home,
  I'm writing it now in a verse,
A menacing terror from Rome,
  A grim Apostolican Curse!

In stern phraseology terse,
  The withering sentence is read,
Recalcitrant minds and perverse
  Are rais'd to the summit of dread;
Then plagued with affliction diverse,
  Till they long for the peace of the dead.

A terrible atmosphere falls
  With dire inescapable spell,
A villainous chill that appals,
  And vile putrefactory smell,
Which ghastly miasma recalls
  The poisonous vapours of hell.

Anathematiz'd by the Pope,
  In Latin or possibly Erse,
I'd lose every vestige of hope
  Through this dark Apostolican Curse,
And look for a suicide's rope,
  Or charter a suitable hearse.

But this was a hideous dream,
  Of days that were wicked and vile,
For Popes it would certainly seem
  Have travelled full many a mile,
All ready the past to redeem,
  With a warm Ecumenical Smile!

... DEF'NITLEE

WHY YES!

I ASKED her if she liked her tea,
  Smiling, she answered,
                        'Def'nitlee.'

It made me glad to be alive
To hear her strong affirmative;
    Not 'Yah,'
        Or 'Yeah,'
            'Yip,'
                or 'Yup,'
Not, 'Sure, I'll have another cup,'
But starkly Latin as could be:
  A tri-syllabic
                        'Def'nitlee.'

Amid this world of flux and fear,
Her 'yes' was absolutely clear:
        No single particle,
                But three,
A firm, resounding
                        'Def'nitlee.'

'Let yea be yea,
    And nay be nay,'
Is language of a bygone day.
Revisers of the N.E.B.
    Write: 'Let your yes be
                        Def'nitlee.'

I rose, suggesting,
    'Shall we Twist'
My sweet instinctive classicist?
Bewildered eyes glanced up at me,
        Yet, still she answered,
                        'Def'nitlee.'

...I'M GOING TO FAINT

SMELLY TELLY

A vicar whose service had been broadcast received an irate complaint from a listener who said that his wife nearly fainted at the smell of the incense.

TURN off the television, George,
I think I'm going to faint,
It reeks of horrid incense clouds,
A nauseating taint.

This pseudo-pious ritual,
This vile and filthy pong,
Impresses me as fatuous
And positively wrong.

I do not mind tobacco smoke,
    The smell of twist or shag,
The reek of paint or petrol fumes,
    The stink of burning rag.

I can inhale the vapourings
    Of chemicals or smog,
Of gorgonzola, stilton cheese,
    Or swill to feed the hog.

But incense always aggravates
    A queer internal pain;
I think it should be fiercely banned,
    Like reefers, or cocaine.

We thought we had evaded it
    By leaving in the lurch
A most insistent clergyman,
    Who swings it round his church.

But this abomination now
    Within the TV lurks,
Exuding vile effluvia,
    And gumming up the works.

The Vicar says, in Heaven above
    There's nothing else to smell;
I'd rather have the brimstone fumes.
    I guess I'll go to Hell.

FRAGMENT

Readers of *A Town Parson's Day* have asked for details concerning the delinquency of 'young Mrs. Brown's turbulent child' represented in the verse by a significant row of dots. Research among the original documents has unearthed the missing passage.

AND now all the terrible tale is revealed:
It seems, Master Tommy, when crossing a field
On the edge of the town, found a series of pens
Containing some rather excitable hens;
And thought it a specially comical joke
To set them at liberty, then to provoke
The fowls to a wonderful Marathon race,
With Ginger the dog taking part in the chase.

Then, seizing a basket of newly-laid eggs,
(A find that for devilry patently begs!)
Young Tommy invented the gayest of larks,
Eggs thrown at a target make glorious marks!

The owner, however, as soon as he knew
Adopted a totally different view,
And, having a feeble opinion of sport,
Announced his intention of going to court.

The consequent trouble may not be so bad
If only the Vicar will speak for the lad. . . .

TAIL-PIECE

A RAVENOUS dog, on the run,
Thought a Feast at a Convent was fun.
   'But it's only a feria,'
    Said Mother Superior,
And so the poor doggie had nun.